STORY AND ART BY

HIDEKI GOTO

Splatoon
SQUID KIDS
COMEDY SHOW

Volume 6
VIZ Media Edition

Story and Art by
Hideki Goto

Translation **Tetsuichiro Miyaki**
English Adaptation **Bryant Turnage**
Lettering **John Hunt**
Design **Kam Li**
Editor **Joel Enos**

Original Design vol.ONE

Printed in the U.S.A.

Published by VIZ Media, LLC
P.O. Box 77010
San Francisco, CA 94107

10 9 8 7 6 5 4 3 2 1
First Printing, August 2022

VIZ MEDIA
viz.com

ratings.viz.com
RATED
A
ALL AGES
PARENTAL ADVISORY
SPLATOON: SQUID KIDS COMEDY SHOW is rated A and is suitable for readers of all ages.

TM & © 2022 Nintend
Splatoon
SQUID KIDS
COMEDY SHOW
6
STORY AND ART BY
HIDEKI GOTO

Characters

Maika
A city girl who uses Dualies.

Kou
An elite boy with three big advantages going for him—he's tall, rich, and smart.

Hit
A boy from the countryside who came to the city to be a cool squid kid!

Contents

TIME FOR A SERIOUSLY SCARY HAUNTED HOUSE!

MODE
TOWER CONTROL
RIDE THE TOWER!
HI, I'M HIT!!
I'M HAVING MY FIRST TOWER CONTROL BATTLE AT WAHOO WORLD!!

AMUSEMENT PARK TOWER CONTROL

SPLATATA...

YOU NEED TO GET PAST THE CHECKPOINTS AND REACH THE GOAL IN YOUR OPPONENT'S TERRITORY!!

THE TOWER WILL KEEP MOVING AS LONG AS YOU'RE RIDING IT.

THE TOWER MOVES THROUGH A LOT OF THE AMUSEMENT PARK RIDES, HUH?
THERE ARE THREE CHECKPOINTS.

WHAT'S THE FIRST CHECKPOINT? A MERRY-GO-ROUND? TEACUPS?
I can't wait to find out. ♪

HAUNTED HOUSE

Haunted House

WHOOO-AAA!! I CAN WAIT! I CAN WAIT!!

BAAAAM

GHOSTS

TMP TMP... TMP TMP...
ARE THOSE GHOSTS?!

DON'T BE SILLY.
SPLATATA
GOTCHA. THEN I'LL DRIVE THEM AWAY!!

FWOOOO...
THEY ARE GHOSTS AFTER ALL!!

Please don't haunt me forever...
IT'S JUST THE OTHER TEAM SPLATTERED WITH INK!!

THE MORE THE SCARIER!

IT'S TOO DARK FOR ME TO SEE WHERE THEY ARE.
LEAVE IT TO ME, MAIKA!!

I CAN USE THE TENTA MISSILES' AUTOMATIC LOCK-ON TO FIGURE OUT WHERE THE FOUR OF THEM ARE!!

THE... *FOUR*... OF THEM?

SHUDDER...
THERE'S SOME-THING ELSE IN HERE!!

GRAVEYARD BOOYAH BOMB

SPLATATATA...
THERE ARE TOO MANY OBSTACLES FOR ME TO GET NEAR THE TOWER!!
All these tombstones...

YOU'RE GOING TO USE THE BOOYAH BOMB TO FORCE THEM OFF THE TOWER!!
KWEEE
GIVE ME YOUR BOOYAHS, EVERY-ONE!!

THAT WAS FAST!! THE BOOYAH BOMB'S ALREADY FULLY CHARGED?!
SHIIING
THANKS, EVERY-ONE!!

THOSE WERE BEYOND-THE-GRAVE BOOYAHS!!

AIIYEEEE...

BOOYAH!

BOOYAH!

BOOYAH!

BOOYAH!

BOOYAH!

BOOYAH!

RIDING THE TOWER

SHH

THEY'VE RETREATED!! TIME TO MOVE IN!!
RRRMBL

Booyah!!
HIT, YOU'RE RIDING THE TOWER TO MOVE IT FORWARD?

HUH?!
I'LL BACK YOU UP!!
SPLATATA!!

WHY'S THE TOWER MOVING WHEN NO ONE'S RIDING IT...?

A GHOST COUNTS AS A SOMEONE!!!
EEEEEK!!
SHFF...

SECOND CHECKPOINT

AVE
MOVE
THE
TOWER
FOR-
WARD!!
DON'T LET THEM NEAR US!!

THE EXIT !!

WHAT'S THE SECOND CHECK-POINT?
THE OTHER RIDES ARE MORE FUN, I PROMISE.

HOORAY!! WE'RE THROUGH THE HAUNTED HOUSE!!
EXIT

IT GETS WORSE !!
SCHOOL OF HORRORS

STILL (AFTER)LIFE PAINTING

WE HAVE TO MOVE THROUGH THE SCHOOL, HUH?
It looks scary.
MUSIC ROOM
THE SCHOOL AT NIGHT IS SCARY...

A GHOO-OST!!
NO, JUST PORTRAITS OF FAMOUS COM-POSERS.

THEY'RE SO REAL-ISTIC AND SCARY.
WE'RE THROUGH THE MUSIC ROOM, SO WE'RE FINE NOW.

AIYEEEEE!!

A MON-STER!!!
HEY! I DREW THAT!!
JUDD
MAIKA

THERMAL INK

IT'S GOT A THERMAL INK ABILITY.

IT'S TOO DARK IN HERE. I CAN'T SEE WHERE OUR OPPONENTS ARE.
SPLATATA...
HIT, USE THIS!!

THERMAL INK?
THE LOCATION OF ANY OPPONENT YOU'VE SPLATTERED WITH INK WILL BE REVEALED.

YOU'RE RIGHT!! I CAN SEE WHERE THEY ARE!!

BUT THOSE ARE NOT OUR OPPONENTS !!

THIRD CHECKPOINT'S THE SCARIEST

WAHOO WORLD IS AN AMUSEMENT PARK BUILT NEXT TO THE SEA.

FWAAAA

THE LAST CHECKPOINT IS THE OCEAN?!

HOORAY! WE'VE GOTTEN PAST THE SECOND CHECKPOINT!!

YEAH, NOW THERE'S NOTHING TO FEAR!!

OK, THIS IS THE SCARIEST PLACE OF ALL!!
ZLLL SSH
THIRD CHECKPOINT:
SALMON RUN, RUINS OF ARK POLARIS

Splatoon
SQUID KIDS
COMEDY SHOW

TIME TO
GO CAMPING ON A
DESERTED ISLAND!

ISLAND NECESSITIES

HI, I'M HIT!!

TODAY WE'RE CAMPING ON A DESERTED ISLAND!!

WHAT DID YOU BRING, HIT?

F-WUMP

THERE'S NOTHING HERE...

...SO I HAD TO THINK HARD ABOUT WHAT TO BRING.

SPLAT CHARGER

BALLER

THERE'S NO ONE HERE TO FIGHT!!

INK TANK

BURST BOMB

BLOBLOBBER

SPLATTERSHOT

SQUID BEAKON

CURLING BOMB

SUCTION BOMB

SPLAT BOMB

They're all weapons!!

FLINGZA ROLLER

ISLAND MEALS

WE'VE GOT COOKING UTENSILS BUT NO FOOD.
LEAVE IT TO ME, MAIKA!!

HIT, YOU'RE USING YOUR SMART-PHONE TO FIND FISH?

I GET IT!! YOU'RE USING A FISH-TRACKING APP!!
41.7 FEET
76.5 FAHRENHEIT
3.5
4.7
7.3
9.2
0
4
8
12
16
20

SORRY TO KEEP YOU WAITING.

Umar Eats

YOU ORDERED DELIVERY BY INKJET ?!

ZWOOSH

BOUNCY SEA

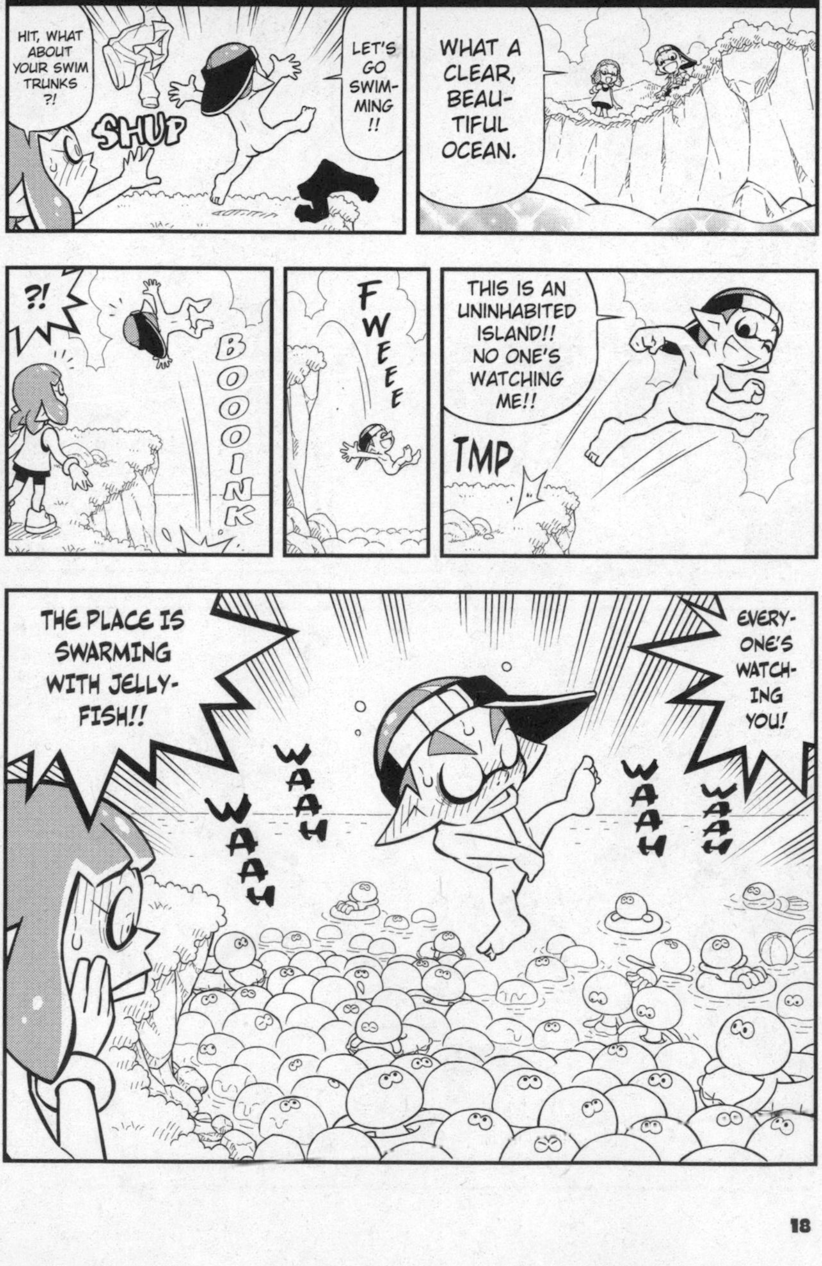

WHAT A CLEAR, BEAUTIFUL OCEAN.

LET'S GO SWIMMING!!
HIT, WHAT ABOUT YOUR SWIM TRUNKS?!
SHUP

THIS IS AN UNINHABITED ISLAND!! NO ONE'S WATCHING ME!!
TMP

FWEEE

?!
BOOOOINK

EVERYONE'S WATCHING YOU!
THE PLACE IS SWARMING WITH JELLYFISH!!
WAAH WAAH WAAH WAAH WAAH

DESERTED ISLAND BATH
I'M TAKING A BATH AFTER OUR MEAL!!
THERE'S A BATH?

ARE WE USING A STEEL DRUM AS A TUB?

IT HAS BUBBLES LIKE A HOT TUB TOO!
BLUB BLUB BLUB
HUH?

SPLISH SPLISH
BLOB-LOBBER
THAT'S A NEW USE FOR THE WEAPON!!

PALM TREE
HIT, A PALM TREE!!
I'M GONNA GET A COCONUT DOWN. CATCH IT, MAIKA!!

BLAM
NICE SHOT!!

A BOMB TREE?!
KA-BLAM
SPLUBT

THREE-FINGERED FOOTPRINT

WHAT ARE THESE ODD FOOT-PRINTS?!

THEY'RE HEADED TO THE TOP OF THE MOUN-TAIN.

A LARGE BIRD?

OR MAYBE A DINO-SAUR?

THE PEAK OF THE MOUNTAIN MUST HAVE A GREAT VIEW, BUT IT'S PROBABLY GOING TO BE A LONG WALK THERE.

WE CAN GO THERE EASILY.

TA-DA! I SET THIS UP YES-TERDAY.
A SQUID BEAKON!!

A WEAPON OF ESCAPE

WE SHOULD ESCAPE FROM THE ISLAND!!
THE INK-JET!!
Umar Eats

I DIDN'T BRING ONE...
THE ONE THING WE NEED!!

DON'T WORRY, WE'VE GOT THE BALLER!!
WE CAN CROSS THE SEA WITHOUT SINKING.

THEY FORGOT ABOUT THE STRONG CURRENT.
PLIP
PLIP

WAITING

THE SHIP HASN'T COME TO PICK US UP.

How about your phone?
It's not charged.
IT'S A LONG DAY.

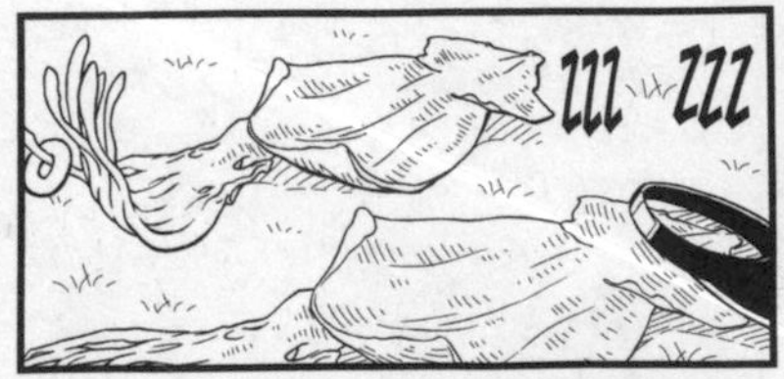
ZZZ
ZZZ

BOMB TREE
PLIP

AH!
WE TAKE ONE LITTLE NAP...!!

LAND HO!

NO ONE'S HERE...
IS THIS ANOTHER DESERTED ISLAND?

WE'RE SAVED!!
SPLISH
SPLOSH
MAIKA, LAND !!

WE'RE SAVED!!
HOORAY! ♪

LOOK!! SOME-BODY'S COMING!
ZLLSH
ZLLSH

WE WERE BETTER OFF BEFORE!!

SAL-MONID SMOKE-YARD

ZLLSSSH

TIME TO SHOW OFF SOME COOL MUSICAL INSTRUMENTS!

RECITAL

TURF WAR! LET'S INK THE STAGE!!
OKAY, HERE WE GO!!

HI, I'M HIT!!
I HAVE BEEN PRACTICING HARD FOR THIS!!
Which weapon is he using?

WHAT?! WHERE AM I?
I'VE NEVER BEEN TO THIS... STAGE...

GYM-NASIUM
IT'S A MUSIC RECITAL!!
MUSIC RECITAL

ARMED AND READY

MUSIC RECITAL
AREN'T WE GOING TO PLAY TURF WAR TODAY?
OH! YOU BROUGHT YOUR WEAPONS AFTER ALL.

AN INK-BRUSH, OCTO-BRUSH...
..AND SPLOOSH-O-MATIC!!

GUITAR

BASS

TRUMPET

OR NOT ...!!

DRUM KIT

WHAT ABOUT YOU, HIT?
YOU CAN USE THIS, MAIKA.
I DON'T HAVE AN INSTRU-MENT...

WHAT IS THIS AWFUL SOUND ?!
THUDD
KLANG
KLAK
CHIK
CHIK
KLANG
KLAK
KA-BLAM
A DRUM KIT!

KA-BLAM
KLANG-KLANG
THUDD
WEAPONS ARE INSTRU-MENTAL!!
CURLING BOMB
SQUID BEAKON
SLOSHER
TRI-SLOSHER
SLOSHING MACHINE

TRIANGLE

HIT AND THE OTHERS ARE PLAYING THE TRIANGLE. I LOVE THE WAY IT SOUNDS.

HUH?! WHAT WAS THAT?
BLAM
KA-BLAM

OH, THEY'RE SPLAT BOMBS !!
KA-BLAM

WAITING

HIT, DO YOU HAVE ANYTHING EASIER TO PLAY?
SURE.

MARA-CAS!!

SPLISH SPLOSH
BUT I DON'T HEAR ANY RAT-TLING ...

KA-BLAM
BURST BOMBS !!
BLAM

ATTACK OF THE SALMONIDS

HALT
THE SALMONIDS ARE HERE!! RUN, EVERYONE!!
OH NO!! THEY'RE ATTACKING THE AUDI-ENCE!!
NO, THEY JUST WANTED TO BE IN THE BAND!!
BOOM
BOOM
KLAK
KLAK
KLAK
KLAK
KLAK
KLAK

HARP

PRRRRM
PRRRRM

HOW NICE. HARPS HAVE SUCH A BEAUTIFUL SOUND. ♥

LOOK, MAIKA.
I'M PLAYING A HARP TOO.

SPLASH WALL
NOT QUITE HIT!

TRADITIONAL JAPANESE INSTRUMENTS

BOOM
BOOM
BOOM
MORE BOMBS ?!

THE OPPOSING TEAM IS PLAYING JAPANESE TAIKO DRUMS!!
They're playing right next to us?

I'LL PLAY A TRA-DITIONAL JAPANESE INSTRU-MENT TOO!!
A BAMBOO SHAKUHACHI FLUTE!!

THAT'S THE BAM-BOOZLER 14!!
SPLUBT

AWARD

DO YOU KNOW ANY-THING ABOUT MUSIC?
JUDD
GOOD GUYS

OUR PERFOR-MANCE WAS NO GOOD. WE'VE PROBABLY LOST...
There's a winner?
WHO'S THE JUDGE?

YEAH!
DID YOU SEE THAT?! WE'VE GOT MUSICAL TALENT AFTER ALL!!
BUT WHY DID YOU WIN?! YOU WERE JUST EXPLODING BOMBS!!

WIN!
BAAM!!
GOOD GUYS

Let's go home.

JUST LIKE A TURF WAR!!

MUSIC RECITAL

GOOD GUYS 24.3%

YOU INKED THE MOST AREA.

TIME FOR A NEW YEAR'S SHRINE VISIT!

TODAY WE'RE PAYING OUR NEW YEAR'S RESPECTS AT SKIPPER PAVILION.
HI, I'M HIT!! HAPPY NEW YEAR!!

HEATED BALLER

WHOA, SO MANY PEOPLE.
MURMUR
MURMUR
MURMUR
IT'S GOING TO TAKE A LONG TIME TO VISIT THE SHRINE... I'M GOING TO FREEZE.

MAIKA, IT'S WARM INSIDE HERE!!
THE BALLER SPECIAL WEAPON !!

BUT HIT, IT'S GOING TO EXPLODE SOON.
KRA-BOOM

IT'S FREEZ-ING!!
FWEEEE
YOU'D PROBABLY BE WARMER IF YOUR CLOTHES HADN'T BLOWN AWAY!!

CRESTED KIMONO AND HAKAMA

YOU SHOULD WEAR SOMETHING SPECIAL FOR THE NEW YEAR'S CELEBRATION TOO, HIT.
A KIMONO LIKE YOU, MAIKA?

GIRLS WEAR A LONG-SLEEVED KIMONO...
...AND BOYS WEAR A CRESTED KIMONO AND HAKAMA.

I LOVE DRESSING UP AS THE SHRINE!

I THOUGHT YOU MEANT FOR THE SHRINE!
ま

FORTUNE

MAIKA, LET'S DRAW FORTUNES!!
WE'LL FIND OUT WHAT OUR FORTUNE FOR THIS YEAR WILL BE.
FORTUNE

WHAT WILL I GET?
GREAT BLESSING? SMALL BLESSING?
SHF SHF
FORTUNE

THIS!!
SHUP
A BURST BOMB?
FORT

GREAT CURSE
KA-BLAM
THAT FORTUNE WAS A BLAST!

BONFIRE

A BON-FIRE!! IT LOOKS SO WARM. ♪
KCH
KCH

HIT, DON'T YOU NEED TO LINE UP FOR THE SHRINE?
SAVE A SPACE FOR ME, MAIKA!!

WE'VE MOVED FORWARD QUITE A BIT...
...BUT IS HIT STILL WARMING HIMSELF IN FRONT OF THE FIRE?

KCH KCH
MAYBE HE'S BEEN THERE TOO LONG!!

WASHING HANDS

ACK!!
Don't fall in the ocean!
BE CARE-FUL, HIT!!

WE CAN'T DO WATER, REMEM-BER?

SPLISH SPLOSH
BUT WE HAVE TO WASH OUR HANDS BEFORE MAKING A WISH!!

WATER
SPLISH SPLISH
I HOPE HE WISHED TO COME BACK.

WARM SUB WEAPON

IT'S GETTING COLD. WE'VE BEEN IN LINE FOR SO LONG...
MAIKA, PUT THIS UNDER YOUR KIMONO TO KEEP WARM.
HIT, YOU'VE GOT A HEATING PAD ON YOU?

THE TORPEDO SUB WEAPON?

I FILLED IT WITH WARM INK.
SHWAAAA
IT'S NOT A HOT-WATER BOTTLE!!

MOVING OFFERTORY BOX

THE LINE HAS SUDDENLY STARTED TO MOVE.

TMP TMP TMP...

IS IT A THIEF ?
THE OFFER-TORY BOX IS MOVING!!

WHAT HAP-PENED?
TMP TMP TMP...
HEY !!

SHFF
IT'S ON A TOWER!!

LONG SLEEVES

WON'T YOU BE AT A DISADVANTAGE WITH YOUR LONG SLEEVES?

I CAN KEEP LOTS OF BOMBS INSIDE THEM, SO NOT REALLY.

TOWER CONTROL

MAKE YOUR WISH ON THE TOWER!

EVERYONE'S FIGHTING FOR THE TOWER!!

MAIKA, BEHIND YOU!!

SWIP

AIYEE!!

LONG SLEEVES ARE THE BEST!!

EEEEEK!! DON'T COME NEAR ME!!

SHOOM

SHOOM

SHOOM

SHOOM

SHOOM

BARRAGE

I JUST NEED TO AIM AT THE TOWER TO LOCK ONTO THE OTHERS.

EVERYONE'S GATHERING AROUND THE TOWER.

WE CAN TAKE OUR TIME AT THE SHRINE ONCE THERE ARE FEWER PEOPLE.

SHOOM

SHOOM

SHOOM

EVERYONE'S THINKING OF THE SAME THING.

SHA

I'LL DEFEAT THE OTHERS BY USING SPLASHDOWN ON THE TOWER TOO!!

OOPS!!

TOWER AND OFFERTORY BOX DESTROYED.

Splatoon
SQUID KIDS
COMEDY SHOW

I wish that we will be
able to pay our respects
at the shrine next year.
Maika

Splatoon
SQUID KIDS
COMEDY SHOW

TIME TO SHOW HOW MUCH YOU'VE IMPROVED!

HI, I'M HIT!!
TODAY I'M GOING TO SHOW HOW MUCH I'VE IMPROVED AT INKOPOLIS SQUARE.

A NEW TURF WAR

TIME TO TRY SOME-THING NEW!
I DON'T SEE ANY INK...
MODE:
TURF WAR
INK THE MOST TURF TO WIN!
HIT, LET'S SHOW THEM WHAT WE'VE LEARNED SO FAR!!

HUH ?!

YOU'VE SET AN INK MINE!
I'LL BE FINE THIS TIME!!

TRAPS AREN'T INK MINES!

INKLESS ROLLER

YOU'RE USING THE SPLAT ROLLER, HIT!
ROLL ROLL ROLL ROLL

ROLL ROLL...
THE INK'S COMING OUT FINE.

THERE'S NO INK COMING OUT OF IT!! YOU WON'T BE ABLE TO INK THE STAGE!!

SEE?

FWIP

A WOOD-BLOCK PRINT?!

The writing is mirrored!!

SHELDON

MY PARTNER, AUTOBOMB

IT'LL TAKE TIME FOR YOU TO INK THE STAGE BY YOURSELF, HIT.

MAIKA, MOVE UP TO THE FRONT LINE!!
SPLATATATA...
I'LL SUP-PORT YOU FROM THE BACK!!

YOU CAN'T DO ALL THIS WITH JUST AN AUTO-BOMB, CAN YOU?
SHA
I'VE GOT A TRUSTY PARTNER.

WOW, DID YOU INK ALL THIS BY YOUR-SELF?!
SPLUBT

YOU TIED A SPLAT ROLLER TO IT?!

TMP TMP TMP TMP TMP

ROLL ROLL...

BEST TIME TO SHOOT

I WAS WAITING FOR THIS!!
HIT'S SURROUNDED!!

I'LL DEFEAT EVERYONE AT ONCE!!
HERE IT GOES. SPLASHDOWN!!
SH
A

PERFECT TARGET
HUNH ?!
SPLOSH
SPLATATA!!!

QUICK MOTION

I CAN'T HIT THE OPPONENT WITH MY BURST BOMB!!

YOU NEED TO AIM QUICKLY WITH MINIMUM MOTION!!
LIKE THIS!!

HUH?! WHAT ARE YOU DOING?

RUBBER BAND
PLIP
YOU CAN'T INK THE STAGE WITH RUBBER BAND GUNS!!

HEALING BEHIND THE WALL

I SET UP A SPLASH WALL, SO YOU CAN HEAL BEHIND IT.
THANKS, MAIKA!!

THEY GOT YOU BAD, HIT.

THEY OPPONENTS WON'T BE ABLE TO COME IN AS LONG AS I'M BEHIND THE SPLASH WALL.

BUT WE CAN STILL SEE YOU !!

FWIP

Why are you changing your clothes?!

ROOM FOR IMPROVEMENT

MAIKA, THANKS A LOT FOR TRAINING ME.
LOOK AT HOW MUCH I'VE IMPROVED!!
YOU'RE GOING TO USE ULTRA STAMP, HUH?
THUNK THUNK THUNK THUNK
HIT, YOU DON'T HAVE ANY INK COMING OUT OF IT!!

LOSE...
WE LOST ...
GOOD GUYS

WHAT?!
AN ORDINARY HAMMER
YOU HAVEN'T IMPROVED AT ALL!!

WE'RE GOING TO CONTINUE HAVING BATTLES!! NEXT, WE'RE GONNA PLAY SPLAT ZONES!!
LET'S ALL HAVE FUN AND IMPROVE OUR RANKS!!

BUT IT'S FUN BEING IN BATTLES WITH YOU, HIT.

THE STAGE WAS DESTROYED BY THE HAMMER.

KRRKT

KRRKT

MY FAULT! MY FAULT!!

KEEP OUT

KEEP OUT

KEEP OUT

KEEP O

KEEP OUT

EP OUT

KEEP OU

HIS RANK IN THE VIDEO GAME ROSE, THOUGH.

Splatoon
SQUID KIDS
COMEDY SHOW

TIME TO GET AN INCREDIBLE PAIR OF SHOES!

HI, I'M HIT!!
I'M BUYING A PAIR OF NEW SHOES AT BISK'S SHOP!!

LIMITED EDITION

WEL-
COME
...
...TO
SHELLA
FRESH.
HEY, BISK.
DO YOU
HAVE
ANYTHING
THAT WILL
FIT HIT?
SOME
NEW LIMITED
EDITIONS
HAVE JUST
ARRIVED.

OH? BUT
I CAN'T
FIND
THEM.
OVER
HERE?
NOPE.

SHINE
SHINE

OH
YEAH...
HERE.

YOU
WERE
WEAR-
ING
THEM!

LIGHTWEIGHT SHOES

WOW, THESE SHOES ARE SO LIGHT!!

THEY'RE MADE OF A SPONGY MATERIAL SO YOU CAN MOVE FAST.

I CAN MOVE FASTER WITH MY BRAND-NEW SHOES!! I'M GONNA BE THE STAR OF THE TURF WAR!!
DASH
TURF WAR

SLOOOOOW
WHAT'S WRONG?
SPISH
SPLISH

THE SHOES SUCKED UP THE INK AND GOT HEAVY...
SHLLRRP
SPONGY INDEED!!

SHOE TRANSFORMATION

I CAN MOVE AROUND EASILY IN BOOTS BECAUSE THEY DON'T SUCK UP THE INK!!
SPLASH
WE HAVE TO CATCH UP BECAUSE WE GOT A LATE START!!

I NEED TO GO TO THE BATH-ROOM...
YOU SHOULD HAVE GONE BEFORE THE MATCH STARTED!!

SHWAAAA
OH?! I'M SUDDENLY HAVING A TOUGHER TIME MOVING AROUND...
FLIP
FLOP

BATHROOM
YOU'RE WEARING THE SANDALS FROM THE BATHROOM!!
FLIP

RARE SHOES

THIS IS COOL!!
YOU HAVE GOOD TASTE!! THESE RARE SHOES THAT AREN'T BEING MADE ANY-MORE.
I'LL BUY THESE!!

TURF WAR
LET'S GO, HIT!!

WHAT ARE YOU DOING? THE TURF WAR HAS ALREADY STARTED.

MAIKA, HOW DO I TIE THIS?
SAMURAI SHOES
WHY'D YOU HAVE TO BUY SUCH OLD SHOES?!

FOOTPRINTS

WHERE'D OUR OPPO-NENT GO?
HIT, LOOK DOWN!!
PEEK PEEK

THE OPPONENT STEPPED IN OUR INK.

SO, WE JUST NEED TO CHECK THEIR FOOT-PRINTS TO SEE WHICH WAY THEY WENT!!

SO... WHICH WAY?
WOODEN SANDALS !!

PERFECT FOR THE STAGE

OUR STAGE TODAY IS NEW ALBACORE HOTEL!!
ARE YOU READY?

I'VE PREPARED THE PERFECT THING FOR THIS STAGE!!

THIS STAGE IS SUR-ROUNDED BY A SWIMMING POOL...
...SO LONG-RANGE WEAPONS HAVE AN ADVANTAGE.

SWIM FINS
FLIP FLOP
THOSE?!

FOLLOW THE SOUND

I CAN TELL WHERE YOU ARE FROM THE SOUND OF THE SANDALS.
KLAKKA KLAKKA
KLAKKA
THE OTHER TEAM IS WEARING WOODEN SANDALS.
KLAKKA KLAKKA KLAKKA KLAKKA

NO!! FROM THE SIDE?!
KLAKKA KLAKKA

WHAT?! BEHIND ME?
KLAKKA KLAKKA

EVERY-BODY IS WEARING WOODEN SANDALS?!

KLAKKA

KLAKKA

KLAK

KLAKKA

SPORTS SHOES

WHAT KIND OF SHOES ARE YOU LOOKING FOR?
WE'RE HOLDING A TURF WAR AT A BALL FIELD.
THEN I'D RECOM-MEND NON-SLIP SHOES.

OUR NEXT STAGE IS GOBY ARENA, THE BAS-KETBALL COURT.

OH?! WHERE'S HIT?
HE WAS SO HYPED ABOUT HIS NEW SHOES ...

BASE-BALL CLEATS
SPIKES FORBIDDEN
I meant ball court.

BAREFOOT

OUR OPPONENT'S USING A BOOYAH BOMB! RUUUUN!!

WHOOSH

THIS STAGE IS COVERED IN TATAMI MATS, SO IT'S EASIER TO MOVE AROUND IN MY BARE FEET.

HIT, YOU'RE BARE-FOOTED?

NEXT, WE'LL HAVE A TURF WAR AT SKIPPER PAVILION, THE SHRINE.

SLOOOW

YOU DIDN'T THINK ABOUT THE GRAVEL!!

OWWW!! OUCH!! OUCH!!

KRRCH

KRRCH

POWERFUL SHOES

51ST TURF WAR
TURF WAR
25 VS. 25
I'M SO SWEATY. I CAN'T WAIT TO GET CHANGED.
ONE MORE BATTLE, THEN WE CAN!!
DASH
PANT
PANT
HALT
SHFF
THOSE ARE SOME POWER-FUL SHOES ...
WE NEED TO GET CLOSER.

SHUP

YOUR SHOES ARE POWERFUL TOO.
WHAT?! THEY ARE?
SHFF
SHFF

POOOOF
POWER-FULLY SMELLY!!
UGGH, IT STIIINKS !!

TIME TO TRY TAKING CARE OF LI'L JUDD!

THE TURF WAR JUDGES ARE THE CATS JUDD...
...AND LI'L JUDD.
JUDD
LI'L JUDD

FIND LI'L JUDD

WHERE ARE YOU GOING, JUDD?
THEN WE'LL LOOK AFTER LI'L JUDD FOR YOU.
MEOW!
I'M GOING OUT FOR A WHILE.

HIT, WHERE'S LI'L JUDD?
WHAT?

HEALTH CHECKUP
WELL, YOU ARE OVER-WEIGHT...

WE'VE LOST HIM ALREADY?!

BAIT

CATS LIKE FISH.

LEAVE IT TO ME, MAIKA !!

WHERE ARE YOU, LI'L JUDD?!

I'M SURE LI'L JUDD WILL COME OUT.

YOU'RE LURING HIM OUT WITH FISH.

WELL, THE SALMONIDS DID!!

CHOMP

ZLLSH ZLLSH

TOWN GUIDE

THIS IS THE WEAPON SHOP. IT'S SHELDON'S PLACE.

THAT'S CRUSTY SEAN'S SHOP.
WANT SOME-THING TO DRINK?

HE'S TAKING LI'L JUDD AROUND ON A TOUR OF INK-OPOLIS SQUARE.

CORRECTION- LI'L JUDD IS TAKING HIM AROUND!!
I didn't know about this place.

DANCING GAME

YOU LOOK AT THE ARROWS ON THE SCREEN AND STEP ON THE BUTTONS BELOW.
Found you, Li'l Judd.

ISN'T LI'L JUDD TOO SMALL TO SEE THE SCREEN ...?

HIT'S GIVING HIM A LIFT.

HE'S GETTING BEATEN UP!!
THUDD
THUNCK
BOOM

SPLASH INTO THE SEA

THIS IS WAHOO WORLD, AN AMUSEMENT PARK...
...WHERE YOU CAN MEET THE MASCOT, FRESH FISH.

YOU CAN CATCH FISH HERE, HUH?
SPLOOSH
OH NO!! LI'L JUDD FELL IN THE WATER!!
SHA
HIT, IT'S DANGER-OUS!!

SPLISH
I died for nothing?!
YOU WERE CATCHING FISH?!
FWIP FWIP
FWIP FWIP

RATTLE

SHFF
SHFF
SHFF
YOU LIKE TOYS LIKE THIS THAT MAKE SOUNDS?
I GUESS YOU'RE STILL A BABY, LI'L JUDD.

SHFF
SHFF
HUH? IT'S NOT RATTLING.

KRA-BOOM
THAT'S A SUCTION BOMB!!

HEIGHT REQUIREMENT

YOU WANT TO RIDE THE ROLLER COASTER?
SHAAAA

SORRY. YOU'RE TOO SMALL FOR THE RIDE.
More than 3'35"

LEAVE IT TO ME!!
NOW YOU CAN RIDE IT TOO, LI'L JUDD!!

ZWOOSH
FRESH FISH MASK
THAT DOESN'T COUNT!!

LI'L JUDD'S WEAPON

HIT, WE'RE PARTICIPATING IN A TURF WAR HERE AT NOON.
I'D FORGOTTEN ABOUT THAT!!
YOU WANT TO PLAY TOO, LI'L JUDD?
YOU CAN USE THE WEAPON WITH ME!!

SHAAAA
HIT'S USING THE INK-BRUSH.

IS LI'L JUDD USING THE SAME WEAPON?!

SHAAAA

NO, LI'L JUDD IS THE BRUSH!

TENTA MISSILES SURPRISE

OH MY!! LI'L JUDD'S CLIMBING INTO A TENTA MISSILES HOLE!!
SHF
SHF

WHAT WAS HE DOING IN THERE?

PHEW, HE CAME OUT.
POPT

WATCH OUT! LI'L JUDD USED IT AS A LITTERBOX! GROSS!!

CHOOM CHOOM CHOOM CHOOM CHOOM CHOOM

LI'L JUDD'S RANK

I'LL PROTECT YOU WHEN YOU'RE IN TROUBLE.
TAKE CARE OF THE INK-ING, LI'L JUDD.

LI'L JUUUUDD !!

OH NO!!
LI'L JUDD IS SUR-ROUNDED !!

SPLATATA...

HE'S SUPER-STRONG !!

SHA

SPLATATATA

THE RESULT OF JUDD'S HEALTH CHECKUP WAS...

OVEREATING
OVERWEIGHT
OVERSLEEPING
4 OUT OF 100

PLEASE GET SOME EXERCISE.

TIME TO TEST YOUR SPLATFEST KNOWLEDGE!

HI, I'M HIT!!
THE SPLATFEST HAS MADE A COMEBACK TODAY!!

WHICH CAME FIRST?

WE'LL SEPARATE INTO THE EGG TEAM AND CHICKEN TEAM TO FIGHT IT OUT OVER A TURF WAR.
WHICH CAME FIRST?
VS
CHICKEN
EGG

WHICH WILL YOU CHOOSE, HIT?
THE CHICKEN CAME FIRST
THE EGG CAME FIRST

BUT THIS IS A DIF-FICULT CHOICE.
WHICH OF THEM CAME FIRST?

I'LL CHOOSE THE EGG FIRST BECAUSE I WANT THE CHICKEN AS MY MAIN DISH.

WE'RE NOT TALKING ABOUT THE ORDER YOU WANT TO EAT THEM IN!!

HOMING SUB WEAPON

THIS SUB WEAPON WILL FIND OUR OPPONENTS AND CHASE AFTER THEM.
Leave it to me!!
WHERE'S THE OTHER TEAM?

TMP TMP
TMP TMP TMP
THE AUTO-BOMB!!

OH?
WHY WON'T IT EXPLODE?

IT'S A CHICKEN !!
CLUCK CLUCK

TEAM BONDING

LET'S GO, TEAM EGG!!
EGGO KOU IS ON TEAM EGG TOO!!

THUNGKT
IT'S KOU WITH THE THREE D'S, FOR DAPPER, DEBONAIR, AND DOLLARS!!
YOU SHOULD GO TO TEAM CHICKEN!!

I SAW MAIKA BUYING A TON OF EGGS YESTERDAY.
I KNOW FOR SURE THAT SHE'S ON TEAM EGG WITH ME!!

HEY, TEAM CHICKEN, I BOUGHT YOU A LITTLE SOMETHING. ♥
MAIKA'S ON TEAM CHICKEN ?!
Home-made egg custard.

EGG-SCAPING OPPONENT

COME BACK HERE !!

HIT, THAT'S THE EDGE OF THE STAGE!!

MAIKA, COME WITH ME!!
WHAT ?!

DID ONE OF OUR OPPO-NENTS GO THAT WAY?

IT'S A CHICKEN !!

BURST BOMB RUSH

KA-BLAM KA-BLAM
KA-BLAM
YAAH, YAAH, YAAH, YAAH, YAAH!!
RUN!! HE'S USING THE BURST BOMB LAUNCHER!!
TAKE THIS, TEAM CHICKEN!!

WHAT?! THEY'VE BEEN STRUCK WITH MY BURST BOMBS BUT THEY'RE FINE?!
HA-HA-HA.
TEAM CHICKEN MUST HAVE BEEN VAPOR-IZED!!

THEY WERE EGGS!!

AUTOBOMB RUSH

YOU'RE NOT USING THOSE USELESS CHICKENS AGAIN, ARE YOU?

ARE YOU USING THE REAL AUTO-BOMBS?

I'M GOING TO USE THE AUTOBOMB LAUNCHER !!

WHOOSH WHOOSH WHOOSH WHOOSH

DON'T WORRY!!

TMP TMP TMP TMP

SEE? THE AUTO-BOMBS ARE CHASING AFTER THEM ALREADY.

TMP TMP TMP TMP TMP TMP

TMP TMP

TMP TMP TMP

THEY'RE CHASING AFTER THE CHICKENS!!

HEAVY DAMAGE

DON'T WORRY!!
IT'S JUST ONE LITTLE BURST BOMB, SO IT WON'T BE THAT SERIOUS.
LOOK OUT!! BURST BOMB!!
SHA
TAKE THAT, HIT!!

WHA ...?!
THUNGK

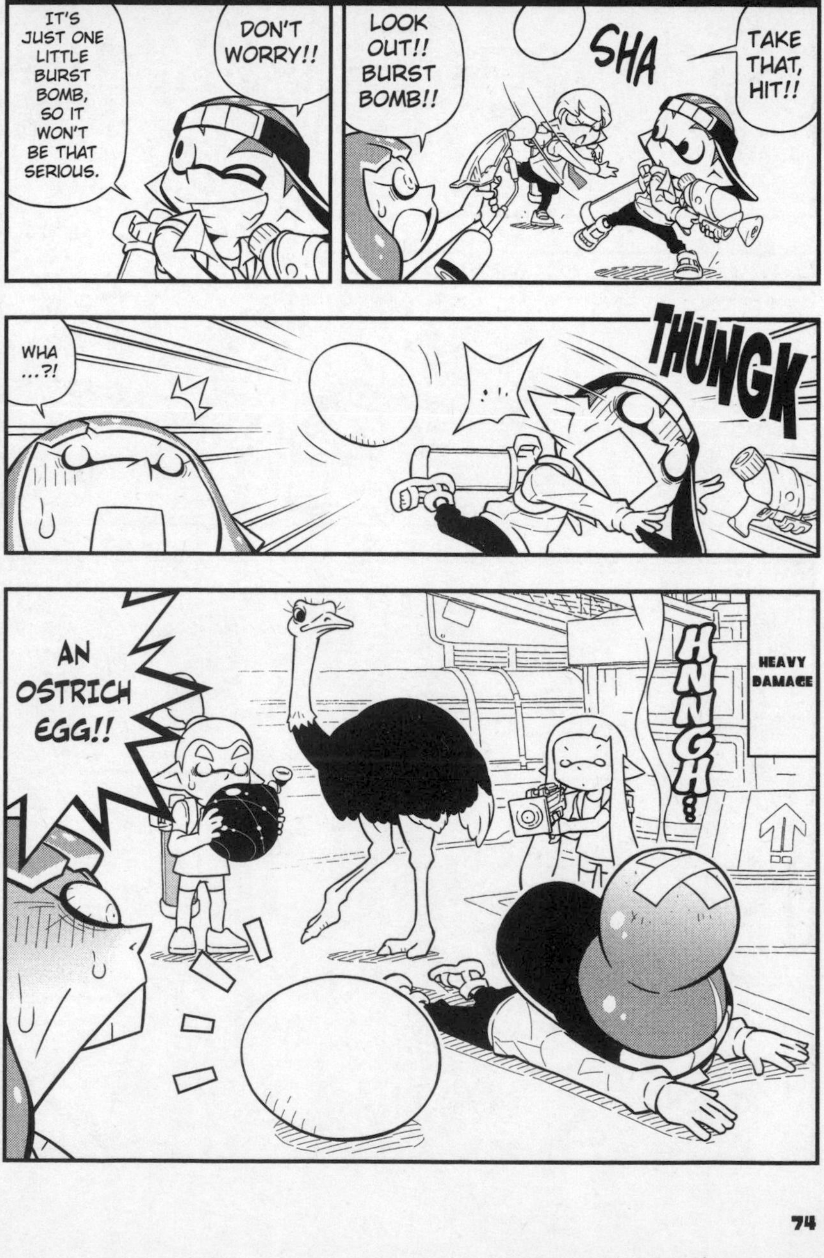

AN OSTRICH EGG!!

HNNGH...

HEAVY DAMAGE

STOLEN BURST BOMBS

MAIKA, WHERE ARE THE BURST BOMBS?
I DON'T HAVE ANY LEFT.

WE HAVEN'T USED THAT MANY.
DID THE OTHER TEAM STEAL OURS?

OUR BURST BOMBS ARE GONE TOO!!
WHERE'D THEY GO?!

THEY AREN'T EGGS!!
WARMING THE EGGS

OBVIOUSLY HIDING

HIT, IT'S DANGEROUS TO BE ALL ALONE AT THE FRONT LINE.

I'LL DIVE IN THE INK AND AMBUSH THEM!!
SPLISH

THEY KNOW?
But how?

THE CHICKEN IS HIDING IN THE INK TOO!!
COCKLE DOODLE DO!

YELLOW WINS

TEAM CHICKEN IS WHITE, AND TEAM EGG IS YELLOW...
Finish!
Finish!
Finish!
BEEEEEP
WHO WON ?!
TOTALLY YELLOW ...
YELLOW
WHITE
YEAH!! TEAM EGG WON!!
HUH?! IS YELLOW MOVING?
GOOD GUYS
BAD GUYS
GOOD GUYS
BAD GUYS
BAAAM
WIN!
CHIIIICKS !!
CHIRP
CHIRP
CHIRP CHIRP
CHICKEN
CHICK
EGG
CHIRP
CHIRP
CHIRP
CHIRP
CHIRP
PLIP
CHIRP
The chickens are laying eggs!!
And they're hatching into chicks!!

Splatoon
SQUID KIDS
COMEDY SHOW

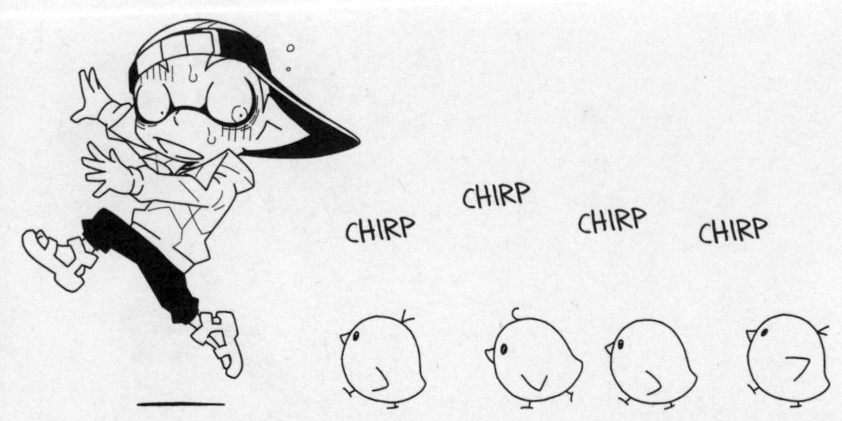
CHIRP
CHIRP
CHIRP
CHIRP

Splatoon
SQUID KIDS
COMEDY SHOW

TIME TO START A PART-TIME JOB WITH EVERYONE!

HI, I'M HIT!!
I'M GOING TO BE WORKING PART-TIME TODAY!!

PART-TIME JOB

HIT, YOU'RE GETTING A PART-TIME JOB?

I WANT TO GET NEW CLOTHES AND SHOES.

I'M GETTING A PART-TIME JOB TOO.

YOU TOO?!

KOU, YOU'RE WEARING YOUR PART-TIME JOB UNIFORM.

IF YOU HAVE ANY QUES-TIONS, MAIKA, ASK ME... THE PRO-FESSIONAL PART-TIMER.

SO, YOU'RE THE LUNCH LADY AT SCHOOL!!

THIS IS A SALMON RUN UNIFORM FOR YOUNG INKLINGS!!

GRIZZCO

YOUR PART-TIME JOB IS TO GATHER POWER EGGS IN SALMON RUN, FREEBIE KOU.
THAT'S KOU WITH THREE D'S FOR DAPPER, DEBONAIR, AND DOLLARS!!
IF YOU WANT TO WORK, YOU SHOULD GO TO GRIZZCO INDUSTRIES.
A GRIZZLY IS THE OWNER?! I WANT TO MEET HIM!!
YOU CAN'T, HIT.

APART FROM JUDD AND LI'L JUDD, MAMMALS ARE EXTINCT.
AND WE, THE CREATURES OF THE SEA, EVOLVED.
THERE'S THE GRIZZLY!!
NO WAY!!

OH, ARE YOU LOOKING FOR WORK?
KR-SHK
IT'S A WOOD CARVING!!

BOAT TRIP

IN ORDER TO GATHER POWER EGGS, YOU MUST GO TO AN ISOLATED AREA INHABITED BY THE DANGEROUS SALMONIDS.
YOU CAN LEARN THE BASICS OF THE JOB OVER THERE.

THEN WE CAN RELAX ON THE BOAT. COULD YOU TEACH ME WHAT I NEED TO DO DURING THE RIDE?

I WON'T HAVE TIME FOR THAT!!

WE'RE TAKING A BOAT THERE.

WHAA-AAT?! BUT IT'S SO FAR AWAY.

SPLOSH SPLOSH

YOU DIDN'T SAY WE HAD TO ROW THE BOAT!!

PHFF

SPLOSH

SPLOSH

SPLOSH

SPLOSH

SPLOSH SPLOSH SPLOSH

KITCHENWARE

THAT'S RIGHT. YOUR JOB IS TO GATHER AS MANY POWER EGGS AS POSSIBLE.
SHOOT THE SALMONIDS THAT COME OUT OF THE SEA TO GET THEM TO DROP THE POWER EGGS.

FRYING PAN
BUT THEY'RE GETTING READY TO COOK. WE SHOULDN'T SHOOT THEM.
SPOON

HIT, THE SALMONIDS ARE HERE!!

THOSE ARE THE SALMONIDS' WEAPONS !!

SLAM

DANGEROUS WEAPONS

DANGEROUS-LOOKING SALMONIDS HAVE APPEARED!!
LOOK OUT, HIT!!

THEY DON'T JUST USE FRYING PANS?!
WHAT'S WITH THOSE WEAPONS?!

HAMMER
CROWBAR
NAIL
CHAINSAW
SHWEEEE

THEY CAME TO REPAIR THE STAGE?!

WHOOSH

KLANG

KLANG

RRRMBLL

Thanks a lot guys!!

NO POWER EGG

NO POWER EGG
SPLATATA...
WOW, IT'S DROPPING SO MANY POWER EGGS!!

I'M JEALOUS OF YOU, MAIKA. I'M NOT GETTING ANY POWER EGGS.
YOU JUST NEED TO SHOOT THE SAL-MONIDS.

SPLATATA
I'M SHOOT-ING THE SALMO-NIDS, BUT THEY'RE NOT DROP-PING ANY.

MALE
SURE, WHY WOULD BOYS LAY EGGS?!

GOLD

GOLD
SPLA TA TA TA
I'LL COLLECT LOTS OF POWER EGGS TOO!!

HURRAY! I'M GETTING A LOT OF POWER EGGS THIS TIME!!
SPLATATA

BUT THE COLOR OF THE POWER EGGS IS DIFFERENT. THEY'RE GOLD!!
ARE THEY GOLDEN EGGS?!

MONEY
IT'S JUST A RICH SALMONID!!

GOTCHA GATCHA

HIT, YOU'VE GATHERED SO MANY POWER EGGS.

WHAT...? BLACK EGGS?!

IT'S SO HARD TO GET GOLD...

I GOT A SILVER ONE, BUT...
WHY ARE YOU EATING SNACKS NOW?!
You want the prize?!
CHOCOLATE
SILVER
PLIP

HOLDER OF THE GOLDEN EGGS

TO BE HONEST, WHAT I AM LOOKING FOR ARE THE GOLDEN EGGS.
NICE. LOOKS LIKE I CAN ASK YOU TO DO SOME REAL WORK.

THE BOSS SALMONIDS HAVE THE GOLDEN EGGS!!
AIM FOR THE BOMB ON ITS HEAD!!

THE GOLDEN EGGS!!
KA-BOOM

SO, THE BOSS SALMONIDS ARE MALE!!
I got it!!
WRONG KIND OF "EGGS", HIT!

QUOTA

ONCE YOU GET THE GOLDEN EGGS, CARRY THEM OVER TO THE EGG BASKET.
YOU TOSS THE GOLDEN EGGS IN THERE.

I'VE ALREADY COLLECTED THREE GOLDEN EGGS!!
I'VE GOTTEN THREE TOO!!
YOUR JOB IS TO MEET THE QUOTA BY GATH-ERING THE GOLDEN EGGS.
LEAVE IT TO ME!! I'LL GATHER MORE EGGS!
What's the quota?

WAVE 1
QUOTA
265240
TALK ABOUT EXPLOITING THE WORKERS!!
We'll never be able to go home!!
Two hundred and sixty-five thousand...

TIME TO GATHER POWER EGGS!

HI, I'M HIT! I'LL WORK HARD AT MY PART-TIME JOB AGAIN TODAY!!
WE'RE GOING TO BE DOING SALMON RUN TOGETHER.

SHIP

IF WE WORK AT GRIZZCO INDUSTRIES, WE'LL BE REWARDED WITH GEAR TO WEAR, RIGHT?
THAT'S RIGHT. I'M COUNTING ON YOU TO COLLECT THE GOLDEN EGGS.

HIT, THE BOAT IS ABOUT TO LEAVE.
OKAY, MAIKA. LET'S HEAD OUT TO THE SALMON RUN STAGE!!

OH? WHERE'S HIT, KOU?
I'M ALL ALONE WITH MAIKA. ♥
A dream come true...

YOU'RE ON THE WRONG SHIP!!

TURF WAR STAGE, MANTA MARIA

LIKE A SNAKE
LOOK!!
THE BOSS SALMONID STEEL EEL!!

AIM FOR THE SALMONID DRIVING IT AT THE BACK!!

IT'S SO... SNAKE-LIKE!
GET BEHIND IT!!

I can't!!
IT REALLY IS SNAKE-LIKE... WITH REAL SNAKES!!

BOSS SALMONID
WAVE1
QUOTA
100
0/4
OUR FIRST QUOTA IS FOUR!!
WE'RE SUPPOSED TO COLLECT FOUR GOLDEN EGGS, HUH?

MAIKA, YOU LOOK FOR THE BOSS SALMONIDS. THEY HAVE THE GOLDEN EGGS.
SURE!!

I FOUND THE BOSS!!

BLUB BLUB
WELL, THIS IS JUST... PEACHY...

DROP TO WIN

SHOOT THE STACKED POTS.

KLAK

SPLATATA...

KLAK

A STINGER!! SHOOT THE POTS DOWN TO DEFEAT IT!!

Okay!!

WE MANAGED TO DEFEAT THE STINGER THANKS TO YOUR ADVICE.

YOU SURE DO KNOW YOUR STUFF, PROFESSIONAL PART-TIMER KOU.

Kou's been defeated too...

THE POTS YOU HIT WERE LANDING ON KOU!!

FLYFISH

THE NEXT BOSS SALMONID IS FLY-FISH!!
KOU, HOW DO WE ATTACK IT?

THROW A BOMB INSIDE WHEN IT OPENS ITS LIDS!!
I HOPE I CAN DO IT.
SHUP

SHA
LEAVE IT TO ME!! MY NAME'S HIT AND I NEVER MISS THE MARK!!

BWUMP
BURNABLE
IT'S NOT A TRASH CAN!!

SCRAPPER

I CAN DEFEAT IT WITH ONE SHOT WITH MY SPLATTER-SCOPE!!
SPLATATA
MY ATTACK'S NOT WORK-ING!!

THAT'S A SCRAP-PER. YOU CAN'T DEFEAT IT FROM THE FRONT!!
ATTACK ITS UNGUARDED BACKSIDE !!

AHH...
BLAM

HUH? I COULDN'T DEFEAT IT...
NOT MY BACK-SIDE!!

DRIZZLER

IT'S DRIZZLER, A BOSS SALMONID!!
MY ATTACKS AREN'T WORKING.
CHIK CHIK
YOU CAN'T ATTACK IT WHILE IT HAS ITS UMBRELLA OPEN.
SPLATATA
ATTACK WHEN IT SHOOTS OUT THE TORPEDO TO MAKE ITS INK RAIN DOWN!!

IT FLIPS OVER FROM THE IMPACT OF SHOOTING THE TORPEDO OUT.

BLAM

SHOOT NOW!!

WHERE'S HIT?

SPLATATA

THUNGKT

THE TORPEDO HIT HIM!!

LOW TIDE

WAVE 3
QUOTA
90
0/6
OH?! WHERE ARE THE SALMONIDS?
THEY AREN'T COMING.

WE HAVE LOW TIDE FOR WAVE 3!!
THE TIDE IS LOW, SO WE NEED TO GATHER THE POWER EGGS OVER THERE!!

THERE ARE SO MANY OF THEM!!
ARE THE SALMONIDS HERE?

SO MANY CLAMS TO DIG OUT.
WE'RE NOT HERE FOR CLAMS!!

GLOWFLIES

WAVE 2
QUOTA
97
0/5
WHAT ARE THESE SMALL INSECTS?!
WAVE 2 IS RUSH, HUH?

THE SALMONIDS WILL RUSH OVER TO THE GLOWFLIES THAT HAVE GATHERED AROUND YOU!!
THE GLOWFLIES HAVE GATHERED AROUND KOU NOW.

ME AGAIN?!
WHY WON'T THEY GO TO HIT?

YOU WANT TO USE IT TOO, MAIKA?
FSSSH
INSECT REPELLENT SPRAY?!
INSECT REPELLENT SPRAY

MOTHERSHIP

HIT THE CHINOOKS HOLDING THE CRATES TO GET THE GOLDEN EGGS.
SPLATATATA
IT'S THE MOTHER-SHIP!!
Up there?!
Where are the Salmonids?
IT'S LOW TIDE, BUT I DON'T SEE ANY SALMONIDS OVER HERE.

IT'S A DELIVERY SERVICE!!

KA-BLAM

Pokuten

amazon.co.jp

FWUMP

FWUMP

Pokuten

REWARDS

I GOTTA SAY, YOU IMPRESSED ME WITH YOUR WORK.
MR. GRIZZ, WHERE ARE OUR REWARDS? THE FANCY GEAR?
Clear!!
x34
x1355
WAVE 1
9/4
GJ!
WAVE 2
12/5
GJ!
WAVE 3
14/6
GJ!
NICE WORK. THAT'S ALL FOR TODAY.

NOW I CAN BE A COOL SQUID KID!!

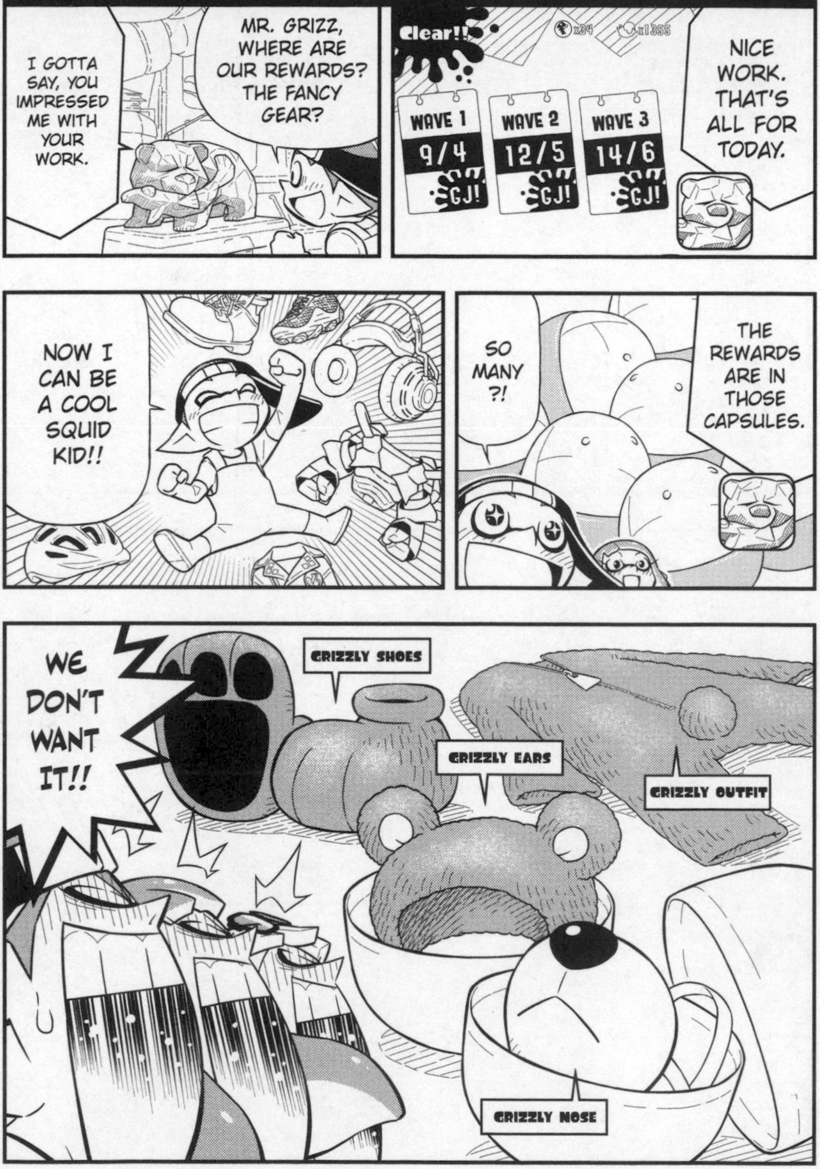

THE REWARDS ARE IN THOSE CAPSULES.
SO MANY?!

WE DON'T WANT IT!!

GRIZZLY SHOES

GRIZZLY EARS

GRIZZLY OUTFIT

GRIZZLY NOSE

TIME TO ENJOY A TRIP TO THE HOT SPRING!

HI, I'M HIT. TODAY WE'RE GOING ON A TRIP TO A HOT SPRING!!

HOT SPRING BUS

MOUNTAIN VILLAGE HOT SPRINGS
POPULAR FOR ALL INKLINGS
INK HOT SPRING ♨
AN INK HOT SPRING !!
WE CAN BATHE IN IT TOO, SO IT'S SUPER POPULAR.
IT'S SO COMFORTABLE THAT ONCE YOU GO, YOU DON'T WANT TO LEAVE.

MOUNTAIN VILLAGE HOT SPRING
MAIKA, THAT'S THE BUS TO THE HOT SPRING!!

VRRROOM
WE'VE BEEN ON THIS BUS FOR EIGHT HOURS NOW, AND WE'RE STILL NOT THERE?

VRROOM

MOUNTAIN VILLAGE HOT SPRING

IT'S SOOO FAR AWAY!!

ANOTHER 15 HOURS TO ♨ MOUNTAIN VILLAGE HOT SPRING

That's why no one wants to leave!!

BATH GOODS

SO, THIS IS THE HOT SPRING INN.
THE OPEN-AIR HOT SPRING IS VERY POPULAR.
MOUNTAIN VILLAGE HOT SPRINGS

FWUMP
HIT, WHAT IS THAT BAG?
MY BATH SUPPLIES!!

THE INN PROVIDES SHAMPOO AND A PAIL FOR YOU.

BLOB-LOBBER
THAT'S WHAT YOU DON'T NEED!!

OPEN-AIR HOT SPRING

MAIKA, LET'S GO TAKE A BATH!!
YOU'RE SO FUSSY. THE OPEN-AIR HOT SPRING IS OUTSIDE.

SPECIAL
OCTOPUS DUMPLINGS
FRIED CHICKEN
WHAT A GREAT HOT SPRING TOWN. SO MANY STALLS.
BATH

I FOUND THE OPEN-AIR HOT SPRING!!
IT'S HERE?!

OPEN-AIR HOT SPRING
THAT'S A TUB... NOT A SPRING.
8,500
8,905
8,905
5,500

BATH BATTLE

LEAVE, HIT!!
I WAS HERE FIRST!!
IT'S THE OPEN-AIR HOT SPRING!!
IT LOOKS GREAT. ♥

YOU TWO BROUGHT YOUR WEAPONS?
TURF WAR
SPLATATA...
LET'S BATTLE FOR IT!
IT'S KOU WITH THREE D'S FOR DAPPER, DEBONAIR, AND DOLLARS!!
THE HOT SPRING IS FOR EVERY-ONE, DORKY KOU!!

THAT'S... DISGUST-ING...!

Shoot, I'm out of ink.

SHWAAAA

EEEEEEK!!

FURRY TOWEL
THERE'S A TOWEL ON THE CUSHION.

MAIKA, THE TOWELS AT THIS INN ARE GREAT.
WIPE WIPE
THEY SEEM NORMAL TO ME.

LOOK AT HOW FURRY IT IS.

THAT'S JUDD THE CAT!!

OPEN-AIR HOT SPRING IN THE SNOW
IT'S SNOW-ING!!

A HOT SPRING IN THE SNOWY OUTDOORS. HOW LOVELY. ♥

EEEEEE!!
A PEEP-ING TOM!!

NEVER MIND, IT'S JUST ALL THE SNOW ON YOUR HEAD!!
WUMP

HOT SPRING CUISINE

DINING ROOM
THIS MUST BE THE DINING ROOM!!
ZWAK
OUR MEAL IS READY.
GRRRUMBLE
I'M STARV-ING.

THEY PROBABLY WANT US TO TAKE A BATH TO RELAX BEFORE THE MEAL!!
SPLISH

A BATHTUB?! A RED AND WHITE ONE TOO.
THE INDOOR HOT SPRING IS OPAQUE, HUH?

AN INN FOR SALMO-NIDS?!

WE ARE THE MEAL!!

KIMCHI HOT POT

SOY MILK HOT POT

Splatoon
SQUID KIDS
COMEDY SHOW

TIME TO USE A CERTAIN ITEM TO BECOME INVINCIBLE!

WHICH POWER-UP WOULD YOU PREFER?
HI, I'M HIT!! IT'S BEEN A WHILE SINCE WE HAD A SPLATFEST!!

SUPERSIZE

TODAY'S SPLATFEST IS "WHICH POWER-UP WOULD YOU PREFER? SUPERSIZE WITH SUPER MUSHROOM OR INVINCIBILITY WITH SUPER STAR?"

WHICH POWER-UP WOULD YOU PREFER?
SUPER STAR
(INVINCIBILITY)

SUPER MUSHROOM
(SUPERSIZE)

WE WILL CHOOSE ONE TEAM TO FIGHT OUT A TURF WAR.

I'LL SUPERSIZE MYSELF WITH THE SUPER MUSHROOM!!
BAAM
BAAM
BAAM

OH NO...

ONLY HIS CLOTHES HAVE SUPERSIZED.

SHUP

NAAAAKED

SUPER NAKED !!

AN INVINCIBLE TEAM WITH SUPER STAR

YOU'RE ON TEAM "SUPER-SIZE WITH SUPER MUSHROOM" TOO, MAIKA?

Let's do our best.

AIYEE!! I'M ON A DIFFERENT TEAM THAN MAIKA AGAIN!!

KOU, YOU'RE ON TEAM INVINCIBILITY?

YES. I'M A SUPERSTAR, AFTER ALL.

SUPER MUSHROOM IS THE BEST!
MODE
TURF WAR
INK THE MOST TURF TO WIN!
SUPER STAR IS THE BEST!!
I'LL SHOW YOU HOW STRONG THE SUPER MUSHROOM IS!!

SHK

SHF SHF

THUD

INK THE STAGE !!

SUPERSIZE INK TANK

INVINCIBILITY IS THE BEST!!
THE BALLER IS INVINCIBLE TOO!!
ROLL
ROLL
ROLL

I JUST NEED TO KEEP SHOOTING IT TO BURST IT!!
SPLATATA
LET'S SEE IF YOU'VE GOT ENOUGH INK.

YOU SUPERSIZED YOUR INK TANK!!
BAAM
HE GOT AWAY. CHASE HIM, HIT!!

I CAN'T MOVE!!
IT'S TOO BIG!!

SUPERSIZE WEAPON

OUR OPPONENTS ARE PROTECTING THEMSELVES WITH INK ARMOR!!

I'LL USE MY SUPERSIZE POWER TO BLAST THEM AND THEIR ARMOR AWAY!!

YOUR WEAPON IS HUGE!!

THAT'S NO GOOD!!
I can't reach the trigger...

TEAM SUPER MUSHROOM

POP POP
POP
POP
LET'S ATTACK THEM WITH OUR SPECIAL WEAPON!!

TEAM SUPER MUSH-ROOM IS USING THE BURST BOMB LAUNCH-ER?!
SHOOM
SHOOM

BONK
BOINK
WHY WON'T THEY EXPLODE?

THEY'RE MUSH-ROOMS !!

NINJA STAR

ROLL
ROLL
ROLL
WE'VE GOT A BALLER TOO!!

SHFFF
I CAN POP IT EASILY!!

Because they're starshaped?
TEAM SUPER STAR CAN USE NINJA STARS?

SPLAT
BONK
IT'S A STAR-FISH!!

ANNIHILATED WITH THE SUPERSIZED BOMB
YOUR BOMBS ARE HUGE!!
DON'T WORRY. WE'RE THE POWERFUL TEAM SUPERSIZE!!
OUR ATTACKS ARE MEANINGLESS WHEN TEAM INVINCIBILITY USES THEIR SUPER STARS!!
THE BOMBS AREN'T REACHING THEM!!
IT'S HEAVY!!
WE'LL BLOW THEM AWAY WITH THESE!!
WE SELF-DESTRUCTED!!
BOOOM
KA-BOOM

FINAL FORM

WHAT WILL HAP-PEN TO THEM?
THE SUPER STAR IS BETTER!!
HUURGH!!
I'LL SHOW YOU THE POWER OF THE SUPER MUSH-ROOM!!

SHII ING
KOU IS SHINING BRIGHTLY WITH THE SUPER STAR?!
HIT IS GIGAN-TIFYING WITH THE SUPER MUSH-ROOM?!
RMMBLL

THIS ISN'T WHAT I WAS EXPECT-ING!!
SHIING
PLUUUMP
NOOOO!

Splatoon
SQUID KIDS
COMEDY SHOW

TIME TO WAIT FOR THE PERFECT PHOTO OPPORTUNITY!

HI, I'M HIT!!
TODAY, I'M GOING TO USE THIS CAMERA TO GET PHOTOS TO WIN AN AWARD IN A PHOTO CONTEST!!

PHOTO CONTEST

I'LL BE THE WINNER OF THE PHOTO CONTEST.

I'M GONNA TAKE A COOL PHOTO!!

HIT, ARE YOU GOING TO ENTER THE PHOTO CONTEST?

I WONDER WHAT KIND OF PHOTOS THEY'RE GOING TO TAKE.
BRING IT ON!!
I CHAL-LENGE YOU!!
I BET YOUR PHOTOS ARE ALL OUT OF FOCUS!!
THE THREE D'S ARE FOR DAPPER, DEBONAIR, AND DOLLARS... NOT DORKY!!
I'LL NEVER LOSE TO YOU, DORKY KOU!!

SO, YOU'RE NOT GOING TO COMPETE WITH YOU PHOTOS?!

BLAM

BLAM

RAIN-MAKER

MAKE IT RAIN!

SPLATATA

I'M GOING TO WIN!!

TARGET

KR-SHK
THEY'RE ATTACK-ING US ALREADY?!
YOU NEED TO BE FIGHTING WITH A WEAPON TOO, HIT.
I'LL GET YOUR BEST MOVE, MAIKA.

I'M SUR-ROUNDED!! HELP ME, EVERYONE!!

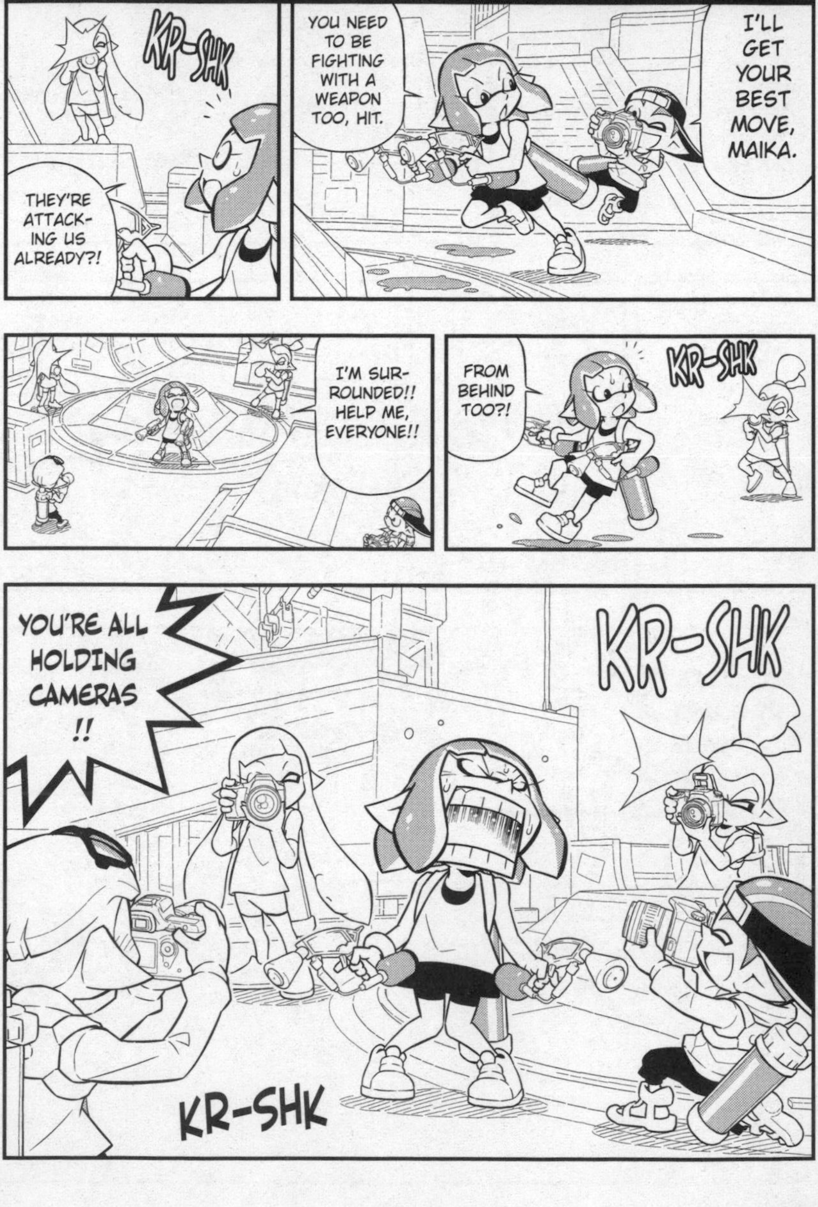

FROM BEHIND TOO?!
KR-SHK

YOU'RE ALL HOLDING CAMERAS!!

KR-SHK

KR-SHK

USELESS BEAKON

YOU'VE SET UP A SQUID BEAKON!!

VSHOOM
NOW I CAN RETURN TO THE FRONT LINE QUICKLY!!

WUMP
WHY CAN'T I SUPER JUMP TO THE SQUID BEAKON?!

IT'S A CAMERA TRIPOD!!
KR-SHK

LONG-RANGE IS OKAY TOO!

BLAM
BLAM BLAM
THE OPPONENT IS ATTACKING US FROM FAR AWAY WITH A LONG-RANGE WEAPON.
I CAN'T REACH THEM WITH MY WEAPON!!

LEAVE IT TO ME!!
I CAN GET THEM FROM FAR AWAY!!

HIT'S USING THE SPLATTERSCOPE, IT'S A LONG-RANGE WEAPON.

PERFECT FOCUS!!
KLIKT
OR A CAMERA WITH A TELEPHOTO LENS!!

FULL MOON
THE MOON IS BEAUTIFUL.
WHAT?! IS THE MOON OUT?
WOW, IT'S SO ROUND!!
WHOA!! THE MOON'S GETTING CLOSER!!
No way!
IT'S A BOOYAH BOMB!!
RUN!!
GWOOOO
SH

OPPORTUNITY
WHERE ARE THEY?
ARE THEY HIDING SOME-WHERE?

SPLATATA

GOTCHA!!
SHIIING
KOU'S ATTACKING ME FROM BEHIND!!

ACT NATURAL, MAIKA!!
KR-SHK
KR-SHK
KR-SHK
KR-SHK
KR-SHK
YOU'RE DOING THAT NOW?!

COUNTDOWN
0:09
0:08
0:07
THE COUNT-DOWN FOR THE END OF THE BATTLE HAS BEGUN!!

WHY HAVE YOU ALL STOPPED?
0:06
0:05
ARE YOU STAND-ING IN THE OPPO-NENT'S INK?
0:04

0:03
HOLD ON, I'LL PAINT UNDER YOUR FEET!!
SPLATATA
0:02
0:01

KR-SHK
IT'S THE COUNTDOWN FOR THE SELF-TIMER!!

CLOSEUP

MY CLOSE-UP PHOTO OF MAIKA ATTACKING IS MORE VIBRANT!!
I GOT AN AWARD FOR THE EXCITING BOOYAH BOMB PHOTO!!

BRING IT ON!!

LET'S SEE IF YOU CAN GET A PHOTO OF THE STRONGEST WEAPON BEING FIRED FROM UP CLOSE!!

THEN I'LL TAKE A PHOTO OF HER FROM EVEN CLOSER!!

A CLOSE SHOT OF THE RAIN-MAKER!!

KA-BLAAM

You're too close!!

KR-SHK
THEY LOST ALL THEIR PHOTOS TOO...

TIME TO WIN THE SPLATOON QUIZ SHOW!

HI, I'M HIT!!
TODAY, I'M GOING TO BECOME A QUIZ CHAMPION!!

INKOPOLIS TRUE OR FALSE QUIZ

HIT, YOU'RE PARTICIPATING IN THE INKOPOLIS SQUARE ULTRA QUIZ SHOW TOO?

I WON'T LOSE, MAIKA. I'LL RISE TO THE TOP!!

DO YOU WANT TO BECOME AN X RANKER?!

Are you looking forward to Splatoon 3?

LOOK AT ALL THE PARTICIPANTS.

QUESTION!! THE TEAM THAT INKS THE MOST AREA IN A TURF WAR WINS. TRUE OR FALSE?!

EASY!! THE ANSWER IS TRUE!!
THE QUESTIONS IN THE BEGINNING ARE EASY SO EVERYONE CAN ENJOY THE SHOW WITHOUT DROPPING OUT.

PLEASE MOVE TO THE TRUE OR FALSE MARK.
WHERE'S THE TRUE MARK?

Ten seconds left.
LOCATION OF TRUE MARK
HE'S PLANNING TO FORCE EVERYONE TO DROP OUT!!

MUDDY TRUE-OR-FALSE QUIZ

JUMP THROUGH THE DOOR OF THE CORRECT ANSWER!!
×
○

QUESTION!! WEAPONS LIKE TENTA MISSILES AND SPLASHDOWN, WHICH CAN BE USED BY INKING THE STAGE AND CHARGING UP THE GAUGE...
...ARE CALLED ULTRA WEAPONS. TRUE OR FALSE?!

A LOT OF CHALLENGERS DROPPED OUT AFTER THE FIRST QUESTION, AND WE'VE GOT NINE PEOPLE LEFT.
You can do it, Hit!!

KRRSH
HE JUMPED INTO THE FALSE WALL!!

CHOOSE THE WRONG ANSWER YOU PLUNGE INTO MUDDY WATER!! THE CORRECT ANSWER AND YOU LAND ON A SOFT MATTRESS!!
THE ANSWER IS SPECIAL WEAPON.

CORRECT!! RELAX AND FALL ONTO THE MATTRESS.

YOU NEVER TOLD ME ABOUT THE FALL!!

FWEEEEE

NUMBER QUIZ

QUESTION!! HOW MANY PEOPLE PARTICIPATE IN A RANKED BATTLE GAME?!
FIND THE RIGHT ANSWER AND SHOOT IT.

IT'S FOUR VERSUS FOUR, SO THE ANSWER IS EIGHT!!
HUH?! BUT WHERE'S EIGHT?
2
4

BLAM
10
6
WHERE ARE YOU SHOOTING, HIT? THAT'S NOT EIGHT!!

DOESN'T MATTER! I DON'T LIKE BEES! IT COUNTS!
THAT'S ONE WAY TO GET AN ANSWER RIGHT.

WRITING QUESTION

YOU'LL NEED TO WRITE THE NEXT QUESTION IN THE PARKING LOT AT MORAY TOWERS.
USE YOUR WEAPON TO WRITE THE ANSWER.

SILHOUETTE QUIZ. CAN YOU CLEARLY TELL WHAT BOMB THIS IS?
MORAY TOWERS PARKING LOT QUESTION

SPLATATA
HIT, YOU'LL BE ABLE TO WRITE FASTER WITH A BRUSH WEAPON!!
SHF

CURLING. CORRECT!!
C URL ING
HE BLOTTED OUT THE QUESTION TO WRITE THE ANSWER!!

SPECIAL QUIZ

THIS IS A BUZZER QUIZ!!
WHAT IS THE SPECIAL WEAPON WITH THE BALL OF INK THAT WILL GROW LARGER WITH THE BOOYAHS FROM YOUR FRIENDS?!
THE BUZZER IS OVER THERE!!
YOU CAN PUSH THE BUTTON BY SHOOT-ING IT WITH INK!!

THE ANSWER IS THIS. BOOYAH BOMB!!
SHWEEE
YOU'RE GOING TO PUSH THE BUZZER WITH THE BOOYAH BOMB!!
YOU CAN REACH UP HIGH AND IT WILL GROW LARGER WITH THE CHEERS FROM YOUR FRIENDS, SO YOU WON'T MISS!!

I'M NOT GETTING ANY BOOYAHS !!
HE DOESN'T HAVE ANY FRIENDS!!

SALMON RUN QUIZ

THE WINNER WILL RECEIVE A PRIVATE ISLAND OF THEIR OWN!! TWO CONTESTANTS LEFT. WHICH OF THEM WILL WIN THE PRIZE?!
MAIKA AND I WILL BE ALL ALONE ON MY ISLAND. ♥
DORKY KOU, IT'S YOU?! I DIDN'T EVEN KNOW YOU WERE HERE!
IT'S KOU WITH THE THREE D'S!! YOU'RE MAKING IT SOUND LIKE NO ONE NOTICES ME!

THE FINAL QUESTION!!
WHAT DO YOU COLLECT IN SALMON RUN?!
WHOEVER BRINGS THE ANSWER BACK FIRST WILL BE THE QUIZ CHAMPION!!
GOLDEN EGGS!! I JUST NEED TO DEFEAT A BOSS SALMONID TO GET ONE!!
THEN THIS PLACE IS...?

THE CHAMPION WILL BE GIVEN THIS ISLAND!!

ISLAND OF SALMONIDS SPAWNING GROUND

ZZLLSSH

I DON'T WANT IT!!

My level in *Splatoon 2* is now 99 MAX with ★ (a star)!! My rank is still the same, though.

Hideki Goto was born in Gifu Prefecture, Japan. He received an honorable mention in the 38th Shogakukan Newcomers' Comic Awards, Kids' Manga Division in 1996 for his one-shot *Zenryoku Dadada*. His first serialization was *Manga de Hakken Tamagotchi: Bakusho 4-koma Gekijo*, which began in *Monthly Coro Coro Comics* in 1997. *Splatoon: Squid Kids Comedy Show* began its serialization in *Bessatsu Coro Coro Comics* in 2017 and is Goto's first work to be published in English.

THIS IS THE
END OF THE
GRAPHIC NOVEL.
TO PROPERLY ENJOY THIS
VIZ MEDIA GRAPHIC NOVEL,
PLEASE TURN IT AROUND AND
BEGIN READING FROM
RIGHT TO LEFT.